Thirty Days of Bible Study for Busy Mamas

# Colossians 3

**Also by Pam Forster:**

*For Instruction in Righteousness*

*Plants Grown Up*

*Polished Cornerstones*

*A Checklist for Parents*

*As Unto the Lord*

*The Virtuous Woman*

*Beauty in the Heart*

Thirty Days of Bible Study for

# *Busy Mamas*

## COLOSSIANS 3

Pam Forster

Doorposts

ISBN 978-1-891206-48-1 (print edition)

ISBN 978-1-891206-49-8 (eBook edition)

Doorposts
5905 SW Lookingglass Drive
Gaston, OR 97119
www.doorposts.com

For Bethany and Susannah

who continue to inspire and encourage me with
their lively, loving passion for God
and His Word

# TABLE OF CONTENTS

# FOREWORD

I remember waking up almost every morning to my mama reading her Bible on the couch. I was completely fascinated by the whole thing – the special colored pencils, the special black pens that she had a never-ending supply of, the pictures and notes she drew in the margins.

I, of course, aspiring to be like my mama and to do this amazing loving-the-Bible-in-a-hands-on-way thing, wanted to draw my own pictures to illustrate what verses were talking about. I can't believe she let me (I would be way too possessive of this gloriously loved and colorful Bible to let grubby little kids possibly mar it with vague scribbly stick figures).

I love that it wasn't just the example of her reading her Bible every morning, but also her including us as she really loved God's word. She inspired me to love my own Bible (and highlight it within an inch of its life!). Reading and marking and really delving into God's word makes it come alive in a way that really changes us. It's not a book to be just read—it's a book to be lived.

My mama is a beautiful, vibrant lover of God and His Word, and I know she'll inspire you to dig deeper and become more obsessed with the Bible. It will blow your mind.

Susannah Forster

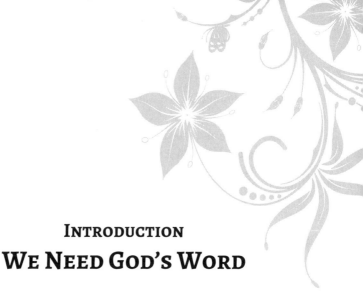

# Introduction
# We Need God's Word

*"Come away by yourselves to a desolate place*
*and rest a while." (Mark 6:31b)*

Do you have trouble even getting a shower, let alone finding the time to read your Bible? This book is for you!

I know that even fifteen minutes of Bible reading and prayer can be incredibly challenging when the house is brimming with energetic children and sweet babies that interrupt normal nighttime sleep schedules. But it is worth fighting for!

Mothering is a demanding job, and it is easy for life to get out of focus if all we see is the diapers and sticky floors and laundry hampers. It is easy to forget Who we are doing this for, and why we are doing it.

It's very easy to become busy, busy Marthas, "distracted with much serving," as we devote our time to the many needs of others (Luke 10:40). We can become so preoccupied with all the demands on our time that we neglect to sit at Jesus' feet with Mary. In doing this, we are in effect saying that we can manage without Him. In reality though, we can't handle this life and its demands all by ourselves.

We need to be in God's Word. His Word is food. His Word nourishes us. Mothers know all about people needing to eat. We hear the words, "I'm

1

hungry," or "What can I eat?" a lot. Sometimes it feels like we spend almost all day planning meals, shopping for meals, cooking meals, serving meals, eating meals, and cleaning up after meals. We need to eat. Without food, we and our families would become weak and unhealthy, and eventually we would die.

Without God's Word we will spiritually starve. We can't just feed on God's Word once a week at church, just like our children can't just eat once a week and thrive. God designed us to need daily sustenance – both physically and spiritually.

There is no way we can raise children who love and follow Jesus if we're not loving and following Him. If we love Him, we'll want to listen to Him. If we listen to Him, we'll love Him even more. And if we truly love Him, that love will spill out onto our children, and draw them to Him in a way that just our words will never do.

A time of prayer and Bible reading acknowledges our dependence on God. Whether we remember it or not, we literally depend on Him for every breath we take. We can't do life without God, so we sure can't be loving, godly mothers without God.

Sitting at Jesus' feet in prayer and Bible study is an expression of our love for Him. We want to spend time with those we love.

When we read God's Word we're listening to our Father, the one who knows us better than we know ourselves, the one who knows exactly how we should live our lives.

God is the source of all wisdom. When we ask Him for wisdom (which we certainly need!), He will give it to us – through His Word and through the counsel of other believers who speak the truths of Scripture to us.

The Bible is the source of absolute truth. It defines what is right and what is wrong. Reading, studying, and obeying it equips us for one of our primary jobs as mothers – teaching and training our children.

Steeping ourselves in the Word equips us for teaching and training our children.

Like food does for our physical bodies, God's Word nourishes us and causes us to grow.

Like sleep that refreshes our bodies, the Holy Spirit refreshes our souls as we rest in the promises of His Word. We won't know those promises if we're not in the Word.

God's Word changes us, and that's what a life of faith in Christ is all about.

A time of Bible reading and prayer gives us an underlying peace in the midst of the interruptions, noise, and challenges that often accompany a house full of children.

Time in the word and prayer strengthens and encourages us and keeps our perspective balanced.

It's not easy – getting into the Word while the house is full of little ones who need us twenty-four hours a day.

But it's essential.

The goal of this book is to offer special encouragement and help to busy mothers who need the nourishment of God's Word in their demanding lives. I want to help you learn to slow down and study the Bible, and then obey it. If you learn some simple, basic study methods, adjust your expectations and goals, and think creatively about times and places to study, I believe you'll get hooked. It's exciting – and fun – to discover the riches of God's Word when we start taking some time to really dig into it.

So let's do it! Let's study together! I challenge you to set aside just five to ten minutes a day – even if it's just one minute at a time – to study the Bible. I'll show you how!

# Day 1:
# Getting Started

We're going to start right out with a month-long series of 5-minute studies on the third chapter of Colossians. For thirty days, we're going to look at just **one** chapter of the Bible and study it, one little step at a time. If you're willing to try for five minutes a day, even if it's in 30-second increments, you will know and understand this one chapter a whole lot better than you did before you started!

**1. Gather the supplies listed below and put them all in one place.**

- Bible, in your preferred translation

- Notebook, small notepad, or even a single sheet of paper — just something to write on. It doesn't need to be fancy.

- Pen

- A computer, or some other device with Internet access. A few of these studies rely on Bible study tools from the Internet. If you don't have Internet access, you will need *Strong's Concordance* for Day 7 and two or more additional Bibles in different translations for studies 17 and 24.

**Other optional supplies:**

- *Colored pencils or pens.* Even crayons would work! We will be marking different words in different ways. Different colors are easiest (and awfully pretty), but don't go buy anything special. If you don't have coloring options, words can all be marked in different ways with just one pen.

- *Computer printout of Colossians 3*, if you don't want to mark in your Bible. You can use www.BibleGateway.com or other online Bible study sites for this.

- *Audio version of the Bible* (or at least Colossians 3), if you want to be able to *listen* to the passage on busy days.

  - Download the chapter onto an iPod or MP3 player at www.bible.is/audiodownloader.

  - Record yourself reading the passage and then listen to it over and over with the *ScriptureTyper* app.

  - Listen on your computer at BibleGateway.com (choose your translation) or Biblestudytools.com (KJV or NLT)

  (See Appendex A on page 71 for more information on pens, pencils, and Bibles.)

## 2. Think about *where* you want to do (or *can* do) your study.

- Is the *bathroom* the one place where you get a few minutes of peace and quiet? Put everything in a basket in there.

- How about in the *kitchen*? Can you squeeze in just a *little* reading while stirring a pot or waiting for the microwave?

- In *bed*?

- In the chair *where you nurse the baby*?

- In the *car*, while someone else watches the kids?

The goal is to think about the place you are most likely to have **5 minutes to read** (not necessarily all at the same time). *If everything is there waiting for you, you'll be much more likely to do your study.* Be strategic.

Keep a basket of playthings for the children nearby, if you'll be doing this while they're awake.

**3. Think about *when* you want to do your study.**

This may not be realistic at this stage of your life, but if you *can* designate a time, you'll be more apt to do the study. Remember, you will only need about five minutes a day. If you want to spend more time, you can, but *five minutes a day is more Bible study than* **no** *minutes a day!* Take what you can get!

- Can you get up just *five minutes earlier* each day?

- Can you talk your *husband* or an *older child* into watching the kids for five minutes sometime each day, or could you do your study right *after the children are in bed* (before anyone thinks about needing a drink or going potty)?

- How about reading *before checking email* or going online?

- Or can you catch five quiet minutes during the *baby's during-the-night or early-morning feeding?*

- Could you start a *quiet time* in the afternoon with all the children on their beds with books or quiet activities? Before you start housework or any other tasks during this time, grab your Bible and do your study!

- Or how about a short *"blanket time"* each morning, with little ones playing quietly on their own individual blankets while you study for a few minutes?

**One of my favorite approaches when our children were little** was to have everyone else pull out their Bible storybooks and have *their own "Bible time"* while I had mine.

Or better yet, *invite your older children to join you!* Read aloud for them, and let them watch you highlight words, or if you're brave, let them do the marking for you!

How about putting digital clocks in the children's rooms? Post a card with "7:00" written on it on a wall near the clock. Explain to your children that when the clock says the same thing the card says, they can get up. Until then, except for trips to the bathroom, they should stay in their beds. Then make sure you start studying by 6:45!

**If you can't do it any other way**, try to grab your five minutes in *smaller snatches,* and put your study materials in the place you're most likely to accomplish that. Do whatever it takes!

OK! We're ready!

You have your materials gathered, you know when and where you would like to do your study.

Tomorrow we start reading!

# DAY 2:
# UNDERSTANDING THE CONTEXT

**Context is important!** If we tried to read just one chapter in the middle of *The Lion, the Witch, and the Wardrobe*, we would not be able to understand the whole story. We could totally miss out on Aslan, or we might think the White Witch was actually good while she was talking to Edmund. We would definitely miss out on the whole triumph of good over evil.

**If we try to read just one chapter of Paul's letter to the Colossians without reading the entire letter, we won't understand the whole story either.** We'll miss out on much of what Paul is saying to the people of Colossae and to us. This letter was written while Paul was in prison, probably in Rome. He addresses teachings that posed dangers to the church and devalued Christ, and he encourages believers to pursue holy, obedient lives in Christ.

**Don't worry when you see today's assignment.** We're starting out with the *longest reading day* of our entire 30-day study. It may take a little more than 5 minutes, but it's only *four chapters long*. After today, we will only be reading Colossians 3 each day.

Don't get discouraged. If you can't carve out enough time to read the entire book all in one sitting, *divide it up*. Read one chapter in the bathroom when you first get up or while you're drying your hair. Read another chapter while you nurse the baby, and another right after you get the kids in bed. Ask your husband or one of the kids to read you a chapter while you cook dinner, or listen to the entire book on your computer or MP3 player as you go through the day. (See Biblegateway. com, Biblestudytools.com, or bible.is/audiodownloader). Be creative!

**If you don't manage to read the entire book,** don't get discouraged and give up after the first day. *We're doing battle here.* Keep fighting. Just *finish reading the book tomorrow,* and then do tomorrow's assignment if you have time. If you get behind, just *keep working. We will have a "catch-up" day every week,* so you'll have a day to catch up! If you get several days behind, just jump forward and join us where we are. The more you can do, the more you'll get out of it. But *do what you can,* and don't give up!

**Assignment:**

Pray for the Holy Spirit to give you understanding and then *read the entire book of Colossians.*

Try to get an overall feel for the *entire message* of the book. What is Paul saying to the Colossians? What is his main message?

If you have time, *assign a title to each chapter* of the book and record it in your notebook. This will help you summarize the main message of each chapter.

Tomorrow we'll start looking in detail at Chapter 3!

# DAY 3:
# IFS AND THENS

**We're ready to start focusing on Chapter 3!** From now on, we will be reading the chapter almost every day, looking for different words and thoughts every time we read.

**Assignment: Read Colossians 3.** Start by praying for the Holy Spirit's guidance. Then, as you read the chapter, use a pen or colored pencil to *circle the word "if"* every time you see it. Depending on the translation you are reading, you should see the word at least *twice*. The NIV only uses it once.

Resist the temptation to skim the passage, looking for the word. Read the *entire chapter* again. Every time you read the chapter, you will become more familiar with it, and that is our goal!

After you have finished finding the "ifs", go back and *read the rest of the sentence that follows the "if phrase".* The word "if" is usually followed by a "then". The actual word "then" is not always there, but it is *implied.*

Here are some simple examples:

- *"If you are tired, you should go to bed."* What does the sentence say we should do if we're tired? We should go to bed. (Sigh. Wouldn't it be nice if we could always do that when we're tired?) The word "then" is not actually in the sentence, but it is implied. If we're tired, *then* we should go to bed.

- *"If you hit your sister, you will be disciplined."* If Daniel hits his sister, *then* he will be disciplined.

Returning to Colossians 3, verse 1 opens with the word "if" (unless you are reading in the NIV). *"If* you have been raised with Christ..."

Look carefully at the verse. If you have been raised with Christ, what should you do? *Underline this part of the verse.* I also like to draw an arrow at the beginning of these phrases. The arrow helps me see the connection between the "if phrase" and the "then phrase".

Continue reading, underlining the other "then phrase" in the chapter.

Go back and read the verses you have marked. Record them in your notebook. *These are clear instructions that God is giving us in His Word.* Think about these commands. Are you obeying them? Meditate on these verses as you go through your day, and ask God to give you the grace to obey them.

# DAY 4:
# CONTRASTS

We're making progress. By the end of the month, in 5-minute chunks, we will have spent about 2-1/2 hours studying this one chapter. I pray you will see that those five minutes a day can make a big difference in your life!

**Assignment: Read Colossians 3.** This time we're going to look for *contrasts* — places where we are told to "do this, not that". Let's look at three examples to help explain what we're talking about:

- *"I would like you to put your shoes on this shelf, not in the middle of the floor where everyone will trip over them."* Do you see the contrast in this sentence? Put your shoes here (on the shelf), **not** there (on the floor).

- *"I would like chocolate ice cream, not vanilla (unless you're going to smother it in chocolate syrup)."* Chocolate, **not** vanilla. Oh, yes.

- *"For by grace you have been saved through faith. And this is not your own doing; it is the gift of God, not a result of works, so that no one may boast."* These verses (Ephesians 2:8-9) contain *two* contrasts. We're saved by grace, **not** by our own doing. Salvation is a gift of God, **not** the results of our works.

As we pray for guidance and then read Colossians 3 again today, we're looking for *sentences where two contrasting phrases are joined with the word "not"*. The ESV version that I am using for my study includes at least *four examples* of this.

**Hints:** One verse is early in the chapter. The other three are all in the last portion of the chapter. In one verse, the "not phrase" comes *before* the phrase that tells us what we *should* do.

As you discover these verses, draw a red X over each of the "nots". Then *record what you find*. Organize these notes in three columns — one for the verse reference, one for what we are *supposed to do*, and one for what we are *not supposed to do*.

Review all your notes. What can you learn from what you have found? *Where is God calling you to grow?* Pray for God to help you recall and apply these truths throughout your day.

## Day 5:

# Putting Sin to Death

Colossians 3 talks about resurrection and death. We've been raised with Christ. We've died and our lives are hidden with Christ. When Christ appears, we will be glorified with Him. In the meantime, we're to put to death our sinful desires.

**Assignment: Read Colossians 3.** We're going to *make a list* today. List everything this chapter tells us to *put to death, put away,* and *not do.* In other words, we are going to list all the *negative commands.* (Next Monday we'll be listing the positive commands — the things we are told *to do.*)

You should be able to find around a dozen negative commands. *Choose a way to mark each of these in your Bible* (or on your printed text, if you do not want to mark in your actual Bible). You might want to draw a simple sword shape over each word, or draw a diagonal slash or horizontal line through each word. Be sure to use a light enough color to allow you to still read the word underneath your marking.

When you are done reading, make a list in your notebook of all the things God, in this chapter, commands us to put away and not do. If you are reading in the King James Version, you may need to take some time to look up definitions of some of the words.

**Review your list.** I don't know about you, but I have definitely not put away — for good — all these attitudes and actions. But praise God! *His Son, Jesus, did!* He lived a perfect life and paid the penalty for my sin. I am in Christ now, and set free from the bondage to sin.

**I don't have to kick myself every time I prove I am still hauling around my old sin nature.** I don't have to be discouraged. I have His Holy Spirit, and He is progressively conforming me to Christ's image. He will work in my life — sometimes in very uncomfortable ways — to make me more like Jesus.

*What sins on your list from today's study are you struggling with most?* Thank God for His salvation and grace, and gratefully submit to His working in your life. He loves you and already counts you forgiven, if you have put your faith in Jesus. Paul assures us of this earlier in the book of Colossians:

*"...giving thanks to the Father, who has qualified you to share in the inheritance of the saints in light. He has delivered us from the domain of darkness and transferred us to the kingdom of his beloved Son, in whom we have redemption, the forgiveness of sins."* (1:12-14)

**We can now bask in the security of that forgiveness.** When we understand our position in Christ and all that He accomplished for us, it will lead us to *love* Him, and when we love Him, we will *want* to please and glorify Him, we will want to put to death sinful thoughts and actions — not out of fear of punishment, but out of gratitude.

## DAY 6:

# PUTTING ON

We've been studying the Bible together for a week now! Isn't it exciting to dig into a passage and really look at it?

**Assignment: Read Colossians 3.** Pray for the Holy Spirit's help as you read the chapter again. It should be starting to feel pretty familiar to you. Mark in a unique way *each trait and action that God tells us to "put on" or do.* We're looking for *positive commands* today.

Note all actions and attitudes in your notebook, along with the references for the verses. *Save verses 18-25 for another day. We will look at those verses separately.* In the rest of the chapter you should be able to find more than a dozen positive commands to list.

*Review your list* after you have read the chapter. These are virtues that God desires to build in our lives. We can't manufacture them on our own. But with the Holy Spirit's help we can grow to reflect the character of Christ. Verse 10 says that as believers, we have "put on the new self, which is being renewed in knowledge after the image of its creator."

In what areas do you need to grow? Which trait can you focus on today? List some specific ways you can "put on" one of these traits. For instance, in what ways can you demonstrate compassion to your children or husband? In what ways can you exercise kindness toward your neighbors or toward others in need? Is there someone you need to forgive? Pick up one of these virtues and *put it on.*

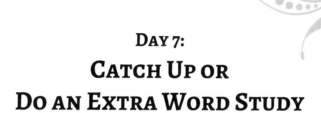

## Day 7:
# Catch Up or Do an Extra Word Study

**This is your day** to *catch up* if you've missed an assignment or two in the midst of diaper changes, dirty dishes, and laundry. If you don't need to catch up, this can be a day to read back through the chapter and meditate on what you have learned so far.

For those of you who have the time, I'll be including optional "dig deeper" type of assignments on our catch-up days. *If you're struggling just to keep up with the 5-minute assignments, don't even read these assignments!* But if you have the time and *want* more, we'll be offering some optional study ideas for these catch up days.

Today we're going to walk through a *word study,* step-by-step, using *Strong's Exhaustive Concordance* online. Our lists that we made on Days 5 and 6 (the sins we are to put off and the virtues we are to put on) give us some good material for potential word studies. Whatever version you have been studying, today we will consider the phrase "bowels of mercies" from the KJV to help us learn how to study more deeply the words used in the Bible. Here's one way to learn a little more about those words.

- Go to www.Biblestudytools.com.

- Then click on "Library" in the upper tool bar.

- Click on "Concordances".

- Click on "Strong's Exhaustive Concordance".

- Type in "bowels of mercies" in the "Search the Bible with Strongs" box and click "Search".

- Click on the reference for Colossians 3:12. You should see 3 check boxes above the verse.

- Check the "Strong's Number" box on the right.

- Click on the word "bowels" in the verse. This will give you the original Greek word that the King James Version translated as "bowels" in Colossians 3:12.

- Read the definition of the word.

- Under "King James Word Usage" we see how many other times this Greek word is used in the New Testament, and the other English words used to translate it. This helps us understand the word a bit better.

- To get an even better understanding of the word as it is used throughout the New Testament, we can look under the heading, "KJV Verse Count". Here we see which other New Testament books contain this same word.

- Before we look at these verses, make note of the Strong's number that is assigned to the word (4698).

- Then click on "Luke". You will see the verse in Luke that contains this same Greek word.

- Hover over the different words in the verse until you find the one that has the same "Strongs number" (4698) assigned to it. This word (tender) is the same word in the original Greek as the word that was translated "bowels" in Colossians 3.

Continue through the list, reading each verse and identifying the word that has the same Strong's number. Reading other verses with the same word (which will often be translated with a different English word in the King James Version) will help us get a better understanding of the word "bowels" as it is used in Colossians 3.

*3628*

If you go through this same process with the word "mercies", you will have an even better understanding of what we are told to "put on" in Colossians 3:12. This process can be used to study more deeply any verse in the Bible. Old Testament verses will be working with Hebrew words, and New Testament with Greek.

NOTE: Because *Strong's Exhaustive Concordance* is an index of all the words in the *King James Version* only, you will have to start out with words *as they are translated in the KJV*. If you are doing your study in a different translation, but still want to study specific words, simply look up the verse in the KJV, and enter those words when doing your concordance search and word study.

**To do this word study without a computer**, you will need *Strong's Concordance*. The steps are a bit different:

- Find *bowels* in the concordance section (in the front) of Strong's.

- Scan the list of verses that use the word *bowels*, and find Col. 3:12.

- The Strong's listing gives the reference, an excerpt from the verse, and a number (4698) to the right of this excerpt.

- Look up this number in the Greek dictionary section (near the back) of Strong's. There you will find a definition of the Greek word and a list of other English words that were used to translate this Greek word in the King James Bible.

# DAY 8:

# JESUS

**The whole book of Colossians revolves around Jesus and what He has accomplished on our behalf!** *In Christ, through Christ, with Christ* — these phrases point us over and over to Him. He has won the battle against sin! With Him, we have died to sin and with Him we have been made alive.

*"And you, who were dead in your trespasses and the uncircumcision of your flesh, God made alive together with him, having forgiven us all our trespasses, by canceling the record of debt that stood against us with its legal demands. This he set aside, nailing it to the cross. He disarmed the rulers and authorities and put them to open shame, by triumphing over them in him"* (Colossians 2:13-15).

**Assignment: Read Colossians 3.** This time look for *all the references to Jesus*. After praying for the Holy Spirit to open your mind and heart to God's Word, *mark each reference to Jesus* with a red cross. Look for any word that refers to Him — *Jesus, Christ, Lord, and all pronouns referring to Him.*

After you have completed your reading and marking, *record everything you learn about Jesus* — what the passage says about Him and about our relationship with Him.

*Review your notes.* Notice how many times Jesus is mentioned in the verses that give specific instructions about how we should live as believers. Why do you think that is? Notice how intimately our lives are linked with His. In what ways should His life impact our lives? What role should the peace of Christ have in our lives? What should we be doing with the word of Christ?

**Let's take a minute here to talk about drawing pictures in our Bibles.** I'm a visual sort of person. I remember what I see and what I write down a lot better than what I hear. So I take a lot of notes during sermons and I write many notes in my Bible.

I've found that drawing little pictures in my Bible helps *stamp truths more deeply* in my mind and heart:

- Thinking about an idea as I draw and looking at the drawing when I've finished *helps me process what I'm reading.*

- Drawing *helps me remember what I've learned* when I open my Bible later and see those little pictures.

- Drawings also gave me *opportunities to talk about the Bible with my young children.* Their eyes would be drawn to the pictures and color, and they would ask questions, giving me a perfect teaching opportunity with a child who was ready to listen.

If you think drawings would help you in your study, take a moment and skim back through your notes from this lesson. Is there a truth that you would like to illustrate? Go for it! It doesn't have to be fancy! Just draw something simple that helps you better remember what you have learned.

For instance, to illustrate verse 15, *"And let the peace of Christ rule in your hearts..."*, I drew a crown with the words "Peace of Christ" below it. I drew some lines radiating out from the words, and then a red heart below the lines. This represents the peace of Christ ruling in my heart.

As you finish up for the day, *reread verses* that stand out to you. Use specific verses as a *prayer* to God (i.e.,"Lord, let the peace of Christ rule in my heart today.") Think of what Jesus has done for you and let that *strengthen and motivate you* as you live the life He has so graciously given you.

**A Project to Do with Your Children:**

*Read Colossians 3 aloud with your children.* Ask them to stand up or raise their hands whenever they hear you say the words *Jesus, Christ,* or *Lord.* (If your children are young, you might want to keep it shorter and only read verses 18-25.) Talk together about what you learn about Jesus as you read. Perhaps you could talk about verse 20, and how their obedience to Daddy and Mama pleases Jesus, or about verse 15 and letting the "peace of Christ" rule in their hearts as they go through their day. Talk about practical ways to do this. Pray together for God's help, and praise them when you see them applying what they have learned!

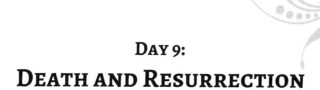

## DAY 9:
# DEATH AND RESURRECTION

Here we are at Day 9 already! If you're in a season of life that makes a traditional "quiet time" difficult, I pray that you're finding that even *five short minutes in the Word each day can make a difference in your thoughts and behavior.*

**Assignment: Read Colossians 3.** We're looking for *three words* today: *Raised, died,* and *above.* Actually, we're looking for those three words and their *synonyms.* For instance, when we look for *raised*, we would also mark *risen* and *rose.*

All three words are not repeated very often in this chapter, but they are important words because of the truths they communicate. *Our whole faith centers around death and resurrection.* We would have no hope, no conquering Savior to put our faith in, if Christ had not risen from the dead.

The three words we are watching for all appear early in the chapter. I chose to mark *raised* with an *arrow pointing up*, *died* with an *arrow pointing down*, and *above* with a *cloud* drawn with a blue pencil.

Mark these three words as you read, praying for the Holy Spirit to make His Word clear to you . Then *reread* the verses that include these words and *personalize* them in your notes. *Rephrase the verse so that it applies directly to you. (*That involves changing second person pronouns to first person pronouns, for the grammar geeks among us.)

For instance, verse 1 says, *"If then you have been raised with Christ, seek the things that are above, where Christ is, seated at the right hand of God."* In your notes, you can write, "If **I** have been raised with Christ, **I** should seek the things that are above."

When you have completed your notes, prayerfully review them, seeking the Lord's direction in your life, and willingly submitting to what He desires to teach you through these verses.

# Day 10:
# Why?

"Why?" Do any of your children like asking that question? Do you ever get tired of answering? *I sure did*, and now I'm getting another opportunity for sanctification with the grandkids' same questions.

We all tend to want to know why we should do something, or why something has happened. Paul does a good job of answering our "whys". In fact, he even seems to anticipate the inevitable "why?" when he admonishes children to obey their parents in everything. Today we're going to look for *reasons* in Colossians 3.

**Assignment: Read Colossians 3** (Again! Are you becoming familiar with this chapter?) Look for all the words that point us to the *whys* of this passage. Look for words like *therefore, since, for, on account of, lest, because, seeing that.* Sometimes the word "*or*" can indicate a reason, too.

*Circle each of these words.* They alert you to the fact that a *reason is being given* for what Paul is saying. If you can rephrase a sentence into a "do this, because" or "don't do this, because" structure, you've found what we're looking for.

Let's look at some examples:

"Don't eat all your candy today, *or* you will end up with a tummy ache."

This can be rephrased to say, "Don't eat all your candy today, *because* you'll end up with a tummy ache."

"*Since* we have to leave for church by 10:30, you need to be out of bed by 9 a.m." We could reword the sentence like this: "You need to be out of bed by 9 a.m. *because* we have to leave for church by 10:30."

"I love Jesus. Therefore, I want to obey Him." I want to obey Jesus *because* I love Him. When "therefore" is used, the reason or answer to our question "why?" comes in the sentence that precedes it.

This one sounds a bit stuffy, because we don't use the word "lest" all that much, but for example's sake (because there *is* a "lest" phrase in at least some of the translations of this chapter): "I'm taking my umbrella along, lest I get caught in the rain this afternoon." Rephrased, this sentence could say, "I'm taking my umbrella along, because I don't want to get caught in the rain this afternoon."

"It's snowing. On account of this, we're canceling school and going out to play." The two statements combined can become, "We're canceling school and going out to play because it's snowing."

*I came up with ten "whys".* See what you can find! As you go back to your circled words, look at the sentences around them. Reword each thought into a statement with the word "because" in it, as we have done in our examples. In addition, when applicable, personalize the sentence by using the word "I" in it.

For example, verses 2 and 3 say, " Set your minds on things that are above, not on things that are on earth. For you have died, and your life is hidden with Christ in God."

To reword this, we would write, *"I should set my mind on things that are above, not on things that are on earth, because I have died and my life is hidden with Christ in God."*

After you have completed this portion of the assignment, take the time to read back through your notes:

- *Meditate on these truths.* Knowing why we are doing something can make a big difference in our attitude while we're doing it.

- Take hold of at least one statement to think about and act upon throughout the day.

- Would it be useful to *write the sentence or verses on a card* to post where you can see them as you work in the kitchen or when you are sitting at a stop light in the car?

- What can you share from this lesson *with your children* that will help them in their walk with Jesus?

Let's be doers of the Word, and not hearers only! (James 1:22)

## Day 11:
# But

"But" is a small word, *but* it matters a lot. "But" changes everything.

Take these verses from Ephesians 2, for instance:

*"...among whom we all once lived in the passions of our flesh, carrying out the desires of the body and the mind, and were by nature children of wrath, like the rest of mankind.* **But** *God, being rich in mercy, because of the great love with which he loved us, even when we were dead in our trespasses, made us alive together with Christ—by grace you have been saved — and raised us up with him and seated us with him in the heavenly places in Christ Jesus..."* (Ephesians 2:3-6)

The "but" in the middle of this passage changes *everything.* We *did* live in the passions of our flesh, we *were* children of wrath, **but** God made us alive. While we were dead in our sins, He made us alive with Christ and raised us up with Him!

Here's another example:

"We were going to stay home all summer, **but** Grandpa just bought us tickets to go to Disneyland." *Everything changes* after those tickets are bought. Instead of staying home all summer, we're going to pack our bags and head for Disneyland. We're going to *do something different.*

It's a good idea to be on the lookout for "buts" when reading our Bibles.

They often carry important messages. Sometimes events are unfolding in a hopeless-looking sort of way, **but** God suddenly intervenes and everything changes. Sometimes someone like David is despairing over his circumstances, **but** then he recalls God's character and promises and, as a result, is ready to trust Him and rest in Him. Sometimes a wayward son is confessing his unworthiness to even be called a son, **but** his father is already ordering the servants to prepare the welcome-home feast.

Things change when we see the word "but".

**Assignment: Read Colossians 3.** *How many "buts" can you find?* In the English Standard Version that I have been studying, I find three. If you're reading in the New King James Version, you'll find more. *Mark each one.* (I highlighted them with an orange pencil in my Bible.)

Then *look at the passage carefully,* asking God to open His Word to you. Each "but" is calling us to think and/or act in a new and *different way.* Pray about these verses and what God is saying to us in them.

Doing something different calls for *repentance* — turning around and heading in a different direction. As believers, we have *"put on the new self, which is being renewed in knowledge after the image of its creator."* (Colossians 3:10). We're being changed. If it's time to turn toward a new way of thinking or doing, commit to doing that now, asking for strength and grace from the Lord who specializes in making all things new.

31

## DAY 12:

# OLD AND NEW MEN

In Christ, we have been made new! We have died with Christ, and we are raised with Christ.

**Assignment for Day 11: Read Colossians 3.** Watch for references to our *old man* or self, and our *new man* or self. Mark these words in your Bible. Then *write a description* of the old self and a description of the new self as they are described in this chapter. Which description fits you best? Are there any old self ways that you still need to put off? Are there any ways you can specifically think of in your life to put on the new self?

**Read the passage again,** this time looking for a *verse that compares one thing to another.* In most translations, this phrase includes an "as" and a "so". (Note: The NIV does not include these words.) The phrase is saying, "just as this happens, in the same manner this also happens." For example:

*"**As** a deer pants for flowing streams,*
*So pants my soul for you, O God."* (Psalm 42:1)

The Psalmist is comparing his thirst for God with a deer's thirst for water. As the deer pants for the water, *in the same manner* my soul pants for God.

The comparison made in Colossians 3 is encouraging us to *look to Jesus as our example.* "As Jesus _____, so you must _____." I chose to mark the "so" in this sentence with two blue parallel diagonal lines //. If we start to understand and truly appreciate what Jesus has done for us, we will be quicker to do the same for others.

Pray for the Holy Spirit to work in your heart. How is He calling you to act "in the same manner" as Jesus did? Write down any specific actions that you believe He is calling you to, and then prayerfully move forward in obedience!

# DAY 13:
# GOD

**Assignment: Read Colossians 3.** Mark in a distinctive way *every reference to God*. Besides marking the actual word "God", mark synonyms also, such as "the Father" and pronouns that refer to God.

In my study, I mark words referring to God with yellow. If I draw a picture to illustrate something about God from the text, I represent Him in the drawing with a triangle, filled in with yellow. For example, to illustrate verse 13, *"For you have died and your life is hidden with Christ in God,"* I drew a red cross (to represent Jesus) and a simple stick figure (to represent me). I colored the stick figure green because I always use green to represent righteousness, and I am righteous in God's eyes because of my faith in Christ's work on the cross. Around the cross and stick figure I drew a triangle and colored it yellow. My finished drawing is a yellow triangle with a red cross and a green stick figure inside it. This represents me *with* Jesus *in* God.

When choosing how to mark different words as *you* read, try to make *associations* in your mind that will help you remember your marking system more easily. The triangle reminds me of the trinity, so that's easy for me to remember. The yellow makes me think of gold, and gold makes me think of God.

Pray for the Holy Spirit's revealing work in your heart as you read. You should be able to find at least *six direct references to God* in this chapter.

*Mark each one.* Then record in your notebook what is being said about God in each verse. When you've finished, take time to look over your notes and meditate on what you've found.

- What does this passage say about *Christ's relationship to His Father? What does it say about our relationship to God,* when we are in Christ?

- How should we *respond to God*?

- What can you take from this reading that will *strengthen and encourage you* in your walk as a believer?

- What can you *share with your children* that will strengthen and encourage them as well?

# DAY 14:
# CATCH UP OR LOOK FOR JESUS IN THE BOOK OF COLOSSIANS

*Today is another catch-up day!* If you've missed some lessons, here's your chance to do some catching up. For those of you who would like more to do, we also have an *optional assignment*.

*Do not do this assignment if you're struggling just to keep up with the five-minute assignments each day.* This lesson will take quite a bit longer, but for those who have the time, it will help you better understand the context of Colossians 3, which will in turn give you a deeper understanding of Chapter 3.

**Optional assignment: Prayerfully read the entire book of Colossians.** *Mark every reference to Jesus* as you read. We've already done this in Chapter 3, so you won't need to re-mark words in that chapter. But it would still be good to reread the chapter, just to understand it in the context of the rest of the book.

Paul's entire letter to the Colossians revolves around Jesus. *I found more than five dozen references to Jesus in these four short chapters!*

*Record all that you learn about Jesus in Colossians.* Then look over your notes. Can you organize what you find into different categories of information? Consider categories such as:

- Who Jesus is

- What His relationship is to the Father

- What His relationship is to creation

- What His relationship was to Paul, the apostles, and the Colossians

- What God accomplished through Him

- What our position is in Him

- How His life affects our lives

This is rich reading! Don't stumble over areas you don't fully understand. It's OK. Rejoice in Christ as He is revealed in this book. Thank God for His Son, and for all the riches that are yours in Him!

*"In him we have redemption through his blood, the forgiveness of our trespasses, according to the riches of his grace, which he lavished upon us..." (Ephesians 1:7-8a)*

# DAY 15:
# VERSE 11

Today we have a study for mamas and also some ideas for *teaching our children* about Colossians 3:11!

Paul reminds the Colossian believers that they have died with Christ. They've also been raised with Christ — raised to a new life with new ways of living. The "old clothes" of their old life need to be discarded. The old sinful habits need to be put to death. It's time to put on their new "clothes". It's time to live as Jesus has empowered them to live. In this new life, the old divisions, the old prejudices, are no longer.

**Assignment: Read Colossians 3:11.** What contrasting pairs of words do you find in this verse? Look up *definitions* of any words you don't understand. (What's a Scythian?)

*Mark each pair of words* in some way. (In my Bible, I marked each pair with a curved line connecting the two words, and then drew a slash through the middle of the line to tell me that they are different from each other.) One pair of words is actually not so different. (When I drew a line to connect those two words, I did not draw a slash through it.)

**Optional:** If you're interested in learning more about this verse (and have *more than five minutes*), this might be a good day to explore a commentary. Instructions for doing that are included in the box on the next page.

*If you don't have time to check out a commentary, simply continue on with the study instructions below the box.*

> **How to use a commentary at *Biblestudytools.com:***
>
> - Go to their site, and click on "commentaries".
>
> - Select a commentary from the list. (I would recommend *John Gill's Exposition of the Bible.* It goes into quite a bit of detail about this verse, but is at the same time very readable.)
>
> - Scroll down to "Colossians" and click on 3, as in "Chapter 3".
>
> - Scroll down to "Colossians 3:11" and click to read the helpful notes on this verse.

Make *a list of the pairs of words* that you have found in this verse. *Think* about your list for a few minutes. What sorts of disagreements and divisions might have formed amongst these different sets of people? What sorts of judgments would they have been tempted to make about each other?

What opposing groups of people could we add to this list in our own present day? *Add these to your list.*

Then, over the top of this list, write the *concluding phrase from the verse*—the phrase that follows the all-important "but" in this verse. (See Day 11.) What do you think Paul is saying in this verse? What is Christ's relationship to all these differing groups of people? If we are *in Christ,* what should *our* relationship to them be? Is God calling you to make any changes in your attitudes and actions toward others?

**For the Kids:** Colossians 3:11 is a good verse to talk about with our children. Children seem to specialize in seeing (and disliking) people that are different than them. They need help realizing that every person they see is created by God and created in His image. They need help learning to love others as Jesus loves them. They need help remembering that the way they treat others is the way they are treating Jesus, because *"Christ is all, and in all".*

We can teach our children this truth in a powerful way by simply re-membering to show *them* love and respect when *they* are "different" than *we* are (and they can be awfully different some times!). Christ is all and in all in *our households*. We should show kindness and respect to our children, even when they are behaving very differently than us, and very differently than we would like them to behave. We should *see Jesus* in every little (and not-so-little) face we look into in our home.

**Read Colossians 3:11 with your children.** *"Here there is not Greek and Jew, circumcised and uncircumcised, barbarian, Scythian, slave, free; but Christ is all, and in all."*

- Talk about the differences between *Greeks and Jews* and the poten-tial disagreements they might have had in New Testament times. (Get help from an online Bible commentary/dictionary, if needed.)

- Explain how early Christians had strong disagreements over *cir-cumcision* and its role in salvation. (Again, get help for this online, if you need it.)

- Look up what the Romans meant when they called someone a *bar-barian*, and find out who the *Scythians* were.

- Talk about the differences between a man who is *free* and one who is a *slave*.

- Talk about how these different groups of people probably looked down on each other, each thinking they were better and smarter and more godly than the other.

- Talk with your children about different kinds of people *they* might be tempted to look down on or make fun of. Help them understand that every one of those people is created by God. Every one of them is created in God's image. Because this is true, every one of them should be treated kindly and respectfully.

- *Get specific.* Does a "different" person live in your neighborhood or go to your church? Have your children been unkind to them, or even simply ignored them? Come up with a plan. What specific things can each of your children do to show Christ's love to that person? What can you do as a family? Do it!

# DAY 16:
# HOLY LIVING

*As we read the third chapter of Colossians, Paul reminds us of our position in Christ. We've been raised with Christ; that's because we died with Him.* So the sins of our old natures need to die, too. We need to put off the sins that we walked in before Jesus saved us. And we need to put on the new garments that Christ won for us on the cross. We are to be like *Him* — compassionate, humble, forgiving.

We're to be like Him, even at *home* — the place where we feel most free to be ourselves — and in the *work place*. That's where our study takes us today.

**Assignment: Read Colossians 3:18-4:1.** Pray for the Holy Spirit's guidance, and then, in your notes, divide a page into four columns. Starting at the left, label these columns "Person", "Do", "Don't Do", and "Why". As you read this portion of Colossians 3, fill in the chart you have made. List the person being addressed, what he or she is told to do or not do, and why.

For instance, verse 18 says, *"Wives, submit to your husbands, as is fitting in the Lord."*

In your chart, write:

- "Wives" in the *Person* column

- "Submit to own husband" in the *Do* column

- Nothing in the *Don't* column (no negative commands are given)

- "As is fitting in the Lord" in the *Why* column

Continue to do this as you read *the rest of Chapter 3* and the *first verse* of Chapter 4. Do your best to put each phrase somewhere in the chart, but don't worry if it's not always completely obvious which column is appropriate. This is just a tool to help you think and observe. You should be able to list six different general groups of people in the "Person" column, along with the corresponding commands given to them.

You should then be able to organize the six categories of people into three pairs. For example, *husbands and wives* are a pair. Each depends on the other. A woman is not a wife without a husband. A man is not a husband until he marries a wife. *Draw a line* that joins "husbands" and "wives" on your chart. (You might want to draw a line connecting their verses in your Bible, too.) Then draw lines to join the other two pairs.

Take some time to *study your chart.*

- What *common factor* exists in each relationship?

- Notice how both people in each relationship are *instructed to behave*. What sort of *balance* has God built into each relationship?

- What are those *in authority* encouraged to do or not do?

- What should motivate those who are *under authority?*

- *What can you learn from this list?* Most of the roles can be thought of in more general terms that apply to each of our lives.

For instance, mothers should also heed the command given to fathers. Employees and wives serving in the home can learn from Paul's instructions to slaves. (Even though these people are not in slave-master relationships, they do have the responsibility of furthering the purposes and goals of those over them.)

**Write down any of the following roles that you have:**

- Wife

- Mother

- Daughter (and daughter-in-law, granddaughter, step-daughter, etc.)

- Worker (in the daily tasks you perform at home, plus any responsibilities and paid employment you may have outside the home)

- Overseer (managing your own household, overseeing children's chores and schoolwork, any other authority roles you have)

Prayerfully review the commands in Colossians 3:18-4:1. What can you learn from these verses that will enable you to better obey God in each of these relationships? Write down specific things you can do.

Then go back and read the *first 17 verses* of Colossians 3. How do Paul's words in these earlier verses relate to his instructions to the family and worker relationships later in the chapter? What can you learn from the beginning of the chapter that will equip and strengthen you to obey God in your roles as wife, mother, daughter, worker, and overseer? *Add these insights to your notes.*

**What is one goal you can set to improve at least one of the relationships listed above?** Write it down.

*Pray over your notes.* Ask God to help you obediently serve Him and others as you seek to apply what you have learned. *Post notes* around the house or *share your commitments* with someone else, if that will help you stay focused.

## DAY 17:
# WORD STUDIES

*Today we're going to do some* **word study**! We'll start with two words from the verses we studied yesterday. Then you can choose any *other words* from the chapter to study on your own.

Let's start with the word "provoke" from verse 21. Even though this verse specifically addresses fathers, the principle of the verse applies to both parents. Mothers might provoke their children in different ways than fathers do, but we definitely are capable of provoking them! So this verse is for us, too! While we're looking at verse 21, we're also going to study the word "discouraged".

To study these words, we're going to use an *online Parallel Bible.* Using this tool, we will be able to read the verse in other translations of the Bible. When we do this, we will see how different scholars translated the original Greek words into English. This will give us a better understanding of both words.

- Go to www.Biblestudytools.com.
- Click on "Bible Study" in the upper menu bar.
- Click on "Parallel Bible".
- Click on the cream-colored box labeled "Compare Translations". (It's near the middle of the screen.)

- Scroll down to Colossians, then to (chapter) 3, and then to (verse) 21.

- When you click on the verse number, it will bring up the verse in a *bunch* of different translations.

Skimming through these will give you a little better understanding of the words, as you see the various ways the original Greek word has been translated.

In your notes, *list the different ways* both words are translated. You might want to also note these words in the *margin of your Bible*.

As an *extra bonus*, the website also includes at the bottom of all the translations, helpful notes from *Matthew Henry's Concise Commentary on the Whole Bible* and from the *Jamison, Faussett, Brown Commentary*.

If you have time, check out the Jamison commentary! It has some *great word study helps*! Their notes on verse 21 certainly convict *me*!) If you have the time, *skim some of those notes* before you move on.

**Assignment: Read Colossians 3.** *Choose three or four words* in the text that you would like to understand better. Write them down, along with their verse references, in your notes.  Following the procedure we just used to study "provoke" and "discouraged", look up the verse reference for each word, and read the different translations. Record in your notes the different ways the words have been translated. *Glance at the commentaries* below the translations and note anything else you learn about your words.

*Review your notes,* praying for the Holy Spirit's guidance. *What have you learned* as you studied these words and read the verses in different translations? *What will you do* with what you have learned?

(If you are interested, Strong's Exhaustive Concordance can be used to trace a word back to its original Greek root and definition. It can also help you locate other places in Scripture where the same Greek word is used [which can increase your understanding of the word]. Day 7's optional lesson explains the procedure for doing this.)

## DAY 18:

# EVERYTHING

**Assignment: Read Colossians 3.** As you read, *circle or mark* every appearance of the words *"all"* and *"everything"*. I found nine occurrences of the two words.

As you find the word, record its verse reference and summarize what is being said. When you have reached the end of the chapter, prayerfully review your notes. "All" and "everything" encompass *everything*.

If *all* of us have sinned and come short of the glory of God (Rom. 3:23), then *none* of us has any hope before God, except through the blood of His Son.

If God works *all* things for good to those who love Him (Rom. 8:28), then *nothing* bad slips past without His approval. *Everything* is ultimately for our good.

If *all* things are possible with God (Matt. 19:26), then there's *nothing* left that He can't do.

*All* and *everything* leave *nothing* behind. Keep this in mind as you review your notes. Do these verses allow for exceptions? Can we keep something back when God asks for *all*? Can we overlook things when God says *everything*?

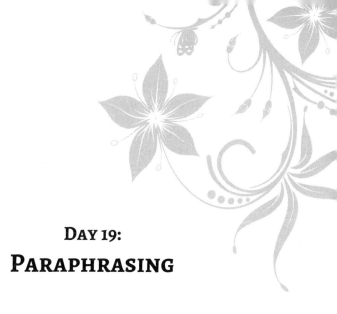

# DAY 19:

# PARAPHRASING

*Let's take some time to summarize* and *paraphrase* what we've been reading for the past two-and-a-half weeks. We're going to put the text into our own words, summarizing as we go. What is the *message* of Colossians 3 and how does it *directly apply* to our lives — now and in the future?

**Assignment: Read Colossians 3.** As you read, *summarize* each main thought and *rephrase* it in a way that puts *you* into the text. In other words, *personalize* the message of this chapter. (This might take more than five minutes. Take heart! Tomorrow is catch-up day. You can always finish then, if you don't have the extra time today.)

To get you started, let's look together at the first four verses of the chapter.

The text says:

*If then you have been raised with Christ, seek the things that are above, where Christ is, seated at the right hand of God. Set your minds on things that are above, not on things that are on earth. For you have died, and your life is hidden with Christ in God. When Christ who is your life appears, then you also will appear with him in glory.*

I have chosen to consider these four verses together as a unit because they are all focusing on the central theme of our position in Christ — our death, resurrection, and future glory with him.

To summarize, and to help me apply the message of these verses directly *to my own life*, I wrote this:

*I've died with Christ. I've been raised with Christ. My life is hidden with Christ. Someday I will be with Christ in glory. So I'm going to focus on heaven, where Christ is, not on earth.*

You may notice that I rearranged the basic content of the passage as I summarized. I did this to help me organize the logic of the verses in my own thoughts. Stating the different aspects of my relationship to Christ helped me better understand *why* my mind should be set on things that are above, heavenly things.

If I've died with Christ and have been raised with Him, if my life is hidden with Him, and I'm going to spend eternity with Him, it only makes sense to be thinking about *Him* and what *He* wants while I'm living this earthly portion of my life.

I also worded my paraphrase of the passage to include *personal pronouns* and *personal commitments*, using phrases like "I am going to". Because of the truth of these words in Colossians 3, by God's grace (with Him enabling me because I cannot do any of this in my own strength), I am going to focus on Christ in heaven, and seek to not let earthly matters distract me from my God-given purpose.

Read through the entire chapter, summarizing and personalizing as you go. Don't stress over this. There's no one perfect, this-is-what-the-teacher-wants way to do this. Your summary of verses 1-4 might look different than mine. The way you group and summarize different verses together may be different than the way someone else will do it. The way you personalize will have its own unique approach, too.

We do, however, want to be careful to *not add thoughts* to the text that are not really there. *We don't want to imply that the passage is saying something that it is actually not saying.* For instance, these four verses are *not* saying that I should just read my Bible and pray ("setting my mind on things above") while I ignore those "earthly" things like mopping the floor and feeding my family. In Christ, those mundane earthly things are transformed into acts of worship, done in service to Jesus.

The point of this assignment is to make the truths of Colossians 3 easier for *you* to remember and easier for *you* to put into practice. Pray for God to lead you as you do this, and savor the time as He speaks to you through His Word.

When you've completed your paraphrase, read back through it, turning it into a *prayer* to God.

# DAY 20:
# MEDITATING AND MEMORIZING

For the past three weeks we've been studying the third chapter of Colossians. Five minutes a day has added up to almost *two hours* now! You might not have time to sit and study for an uninterrupted hour everyday in this season of your life. But five minutes a day can probably happen — even if you have to hide in the bathroom to get it. I hope you're seeing that even that short commitment of time can make a big difference in your life!

**Assignment: Memorize at least one verse from Colossians 3.** You're probably becoming pretty familiar with this text by now! It won't take very long to memorize a portion, or at least a verse or two, from this chapter.

As you read the entire third chapter of Colossians, *select a verse or passage* that you would like to *memorize. Copy those verses* onto several 3 x 5 cards (or ask one of your children to copy them for you), or print them out from your computer. Place copies of your verses in strategic places where you'll be spending a lot of your time — in the kitchen, the car, your purse. Write the passage in a note on your phone, or download just those verses so you can listen to them over and over in a rare quiet moment. Write them with lipstick (an old color you don't like anymore) at the top of your mirror. Whatever it takes! Surround yourself with these verses, and you *will* get them memorized!

Read them often. Think about them. Ask yourself if there are specific ways you can apply them in your life.

*"I have stored up your word in my heart, that I might not sin against you." (Psalm 119:11)*

# DAY 21:
# CATCH UP DAY, PLUS AN OPTIONAL ASSIGNMENT

*Woo-hoo!* It's catch up day! I've given you quite a bit to do the last few days. I'm afraid some of it has probably exceeded the 5-minutes I promised. I'm sorry! There's just so much to look at in this chapter.

But today you have at least five more minutes to catch up. If you need more than that, maybe Daddy could watch the kids for a bit this evening, while you finish up. Or let one cleaning job go for just today, while you make the most of the children's naptime. Or — just pick up where we are now, and don't worry about catching up! It's OK!

**If, and only if, you** *want* **or** *need* **a new assignment for today, try this:**

**Read Colossians 3** (or the entire book of Colossians, if you have time), thinking of it as the *letter* that Paul wrote to new Christians — new Christians who were in danger of being led astray by teaching that would dilute their focus. Put yourself in the place of the Colossian believers, and listen to Paul's warnings and encouragement as you read.

# DAY 22:
# GIVING THANKS

*"He who did not spare his own Son but gave him up for us all, how will he not also with him graciously give us all things?" (Romans 8:32)*

We have so much to be thankful *for...*

...and as *"God's chosen ones, holy and beloved"*, we know Who to be thankful *to.*

Today we're going to look at just *three verses* from Colossians 3. All three of these verses talk about *being thankful.*

**Assignment: Read Colossians 3:15-17.**

*Mark*, every appearance of the words *"thanks"*, *"thanksgiving"*, or any other synonym of the word. You should be able to find three instances of this word. (For those using KJV or NKJV, include the word "grace" as a synonym for "thankfulness".)

Then note what *prepositions* (in, for, to, etc.) follow the word. *Circle those prepositions.* (One occurrence of the word is not followed by any preposition.)

In your notes, *record each phrase* from these three verses that includes "thanks" (and its synonyms).

Meditate on this central portion of Colossians 3, and answer these questions:

- *Why* are we to be thankful?

- *What* are we to be thankful *for*?

- *Who* are we to be thankful *to*?

- *Who* are we to be thankful *with*?

- *Who* are we to be thankful *through*?

- *How* are we to demonstrate and express our thankfulness?

Let these truths bathe your thoughts on this day that God has so graciously given us.

**For the children:**

Take some time during the day *to thank God for His many blessings and for His Son.* Help the children think about things they are thankful for. Then pray together as a family, giving thanks *to* God *for* His blessings.

*"...give thanks in all circumstances; for this is the will of God in Christ Jesus for you." (1 Thessalonians 5:18)*

# DAY 23:
# OBEYING

Let's focus today on *living what we've learned* over the past three weeks. The daily challenges of life, along with the bigger challenges, give us plenty of opportunities to live like Jesus.

**Assignment: Read Colossians 3.** *Pick at least one command* that you want to focus on obeying throughout the day. *Pray about this.* Is God leading you to change and grow in a particular area? If you want, write the command or thought on some cards to post in places where you will be sure to see them.

*Start your day with prayer*, asking God to help you, and continue to pray throughout the day. If you're really wanting to grow, ask Him to *give you opportunities* to apply what you've been learning. He'll be faithful to answer your prayers! Don't be discouraged when you slip. Get up, confess, and move on, remembering that you have died and your life is hidden in *Christ* — the One who lived a perfect life on your behalf.

# DAY 24:
# DIFFERENT TRANSLATIONS

**We've read Colossians 3 almost two dozen times now!** It's time to read it in a *different translation*. Even if you usually prefer one particular translation for your reading and study, occasionally reading in a different version can be helpful. Different translators make slightly different choices of words and sentence structures. Those little differences sometimes give us a fresh look at a passage, or open up a new insight we hadn't seen before.

On Day 17, we used an online *parallel Bible* to help us study particular words. Today we will use that same parallel Bible to look at *two different translations* that are different than what you normally read.

- Go to www.Biblestudytools.com.

- Click on "Bible Study" in the upper menu bar.

- Click on "Parallel Bible".

- In the blue box labeled "Search Online Parallel Bible", type in "Colossians 3".

- In the two gray boxes below that box, you have the option of selecting two different translations to read and compare.

- Make your selections, click "Search", and the two translations will come up for you to read.

Pray for the Holy Spirit's guidance. *Then read both of these different translations.* After reading your normal translation as many times as you have over the past two-and-a-half weeks, you will probably notice a few differences.

For instance, verses 10 and 11 in the *New American Standard Bible*, read like this:

*"...and have put on the new self who is being renewed to a true knowledge according to the image of the One who created him — a renewal in which there is no distinction between Greek and Jew, circumcised and uncircumcised, barbarian, Scythian, slave, and freeman, but Christ is all, and in all."*

The differences in this compared to the ESV that I've been studying are small, but they caught my attention and led me to think about the verses in a slightly different way.

This version refers to the new self with the pronoun *who* instead of *which* like it is in the ESV (*and have put on the new self* **who** *is being renewed...*). That caught my attention. The new self is a *person*, it's *me*, not just something I put on the *outside* of me.

Verse 11 is also easier to understand the way it is worded. The phrase "in which there is no distinction," made the meaning of the verse clearer to me.

As *you* read, record in your notebook any new thoughts or insights from the chapter.

# DAY 25:

# VERBS

It's grammar time! Today we're going to look for *verbs*. Tomorrow we'll look at those verbs in more detail. If you get anxious when you think about grammar, try to stick with me for now. You don't have to worry about getting everything perfect. No one is correcting your work, and no one will ever know if you miss a couple verbs.

**Assignment: Read Colossians 3.** As you read, watch for *verbs* — action words and linking or helping verbs like *is, was, were, have been, am, are,* etc. *Circle each verb and verb phrase.* (Words that precede the main verb often function as part of the verb.)

*Let's look at some examples.* The verb or verb phrase in each sentence is underlined.

- The dog <u>has been digging</u> in the flower bed again.

- The girls <u>are</u> excited about their new kitten.

- <u>Think</u> about what you <u>are saying</u>.

- She <u>is going to be baptized</u> next Sunday. (Actually, I'm not so sure about this one. Is "baptized" part of the verb or not? For our purposes, let's put it in there. It's not going to hurt what we're doing if it's actually a predicative adjective or something instead of part of the verb!)

- We <u>went swimming</u> already.

- <u>Let</u> the bicycle <u>go</u> around you.

- We <u>will be leaving</u> soon.

Ask the Holy Spirit to help you see and understand as you read and as you circle each verb in the chapter. It's easy to miss some, so you might want to skim through the chapter more than once. (And if you miss a few, no problem. You'll benefit from studying *any* of the verbs you find.)

*Tomorrow we will be organizing these verbs into categories.* For today, look over the text with all your circled verbs. Notice the verbs that relate to *Jesus*. Notice how many verbs are speaking *about believers* and how many are *direct commands* to us, telling us how we should live and behave.

Grab one of those commands and put it into action today! We'll finish this verb study tomorrow!

# DAY 26:
# PAST, PRESENT, AND FUTURE

We're going to look at *verb tenses* today! Verb tenses might sound complicated, if you're not a grammar geek. But it's not as bad as it sounds. As we read Colossians 3, we are just going to be noting whether something *has already happened*, if it is *happening now*, or if it's *going to happen*.

If you didn't complete the lesson for Day 25, you will need to do that first. We will be referring to the verbs that we circled while doing that lesson.

In your notebook, draw *three columns*. Above one, write "Past", above the next, "Present", and above the third, "Future". You will be using these to organize all the verbs you have found.

Let's look again at the sentences we talked about yesterday. This time we are going to decide *when* the action of the verb is taking place — in the *past*, in the *present*, or in the *future*. (For you grammar lovers, we're keeping this simple. Don't worry about present perfect, pluperfect, and all that stuff. We're just talking about plain and simple past, present, and future.)

- The dog has been digging in the flower bed again. (He's *been* digging. He's not doing it now. He already did in the *past*.)

- The girls are excited about their new kitten. (They're excited right now, in the *present.*)

- Think about what you are saying. (Think about what you *are* saying — now — in the *present.*)

- She is going to be baptized next Sunday. (*Next* Sunday, in the *future*)

- We went swimming already. (We already went, in the *past.*)

- Let the bicycle go around you. (The bicycle needs to go around you *now*, in the *present.*)

- We will be leaving soon. (We're not leaving now. We will in the *future.*)

**Assignment: Read Colossians 3.** Look at *each verb* you have circled. Place each one, along with the rest of the thought being expressed, under the *appropriate column* — past, present or future — in your notes.

For example, my first phrase in the "Past" column is, "I have been raised up with Christ." My first entry in the "Present" column is, "Seek the things that are above," and my second is, "Christ is above".

Do this with each verb you have circled in the chapter. (This will probably take longer than five minutes. You have another catch up day coming up soon, if you don't finish this today.) Don't worry if you get stuck on a word. Do what you can and don't stress over the ones you can't decipher.

When you have finished, prayerfully *review your lists* and *summarize* what you see.

- What, according to this chapter, *used to happen or has already happened?*

- What actions *have been completed?*

- What *will happen* in the future?

- How should *events of the past* affect our thoughts and actions now?

- How should *promises of the future* affect our present actions and attitudes?

- What is God saying is true about *right now*?

- What is He calling us to do with *this time*?

- Circle any actions in your "Present" column that you need to more faithfully *do*.

- Circle any stated facts in your "Present" column that you need to better *remember and believe.*

- Circle those truths in your "Past" column that you need to better *remember and believe.*

- Circle any promises in your "Future" column that you need to *more fully trust.*

*Pray* for a heart to obey what God *has told you to do*, the grace to remember and rest in what He *has already done*, and the faith to believe in what He *has promised to do*.

## DAY 27:

# ORGANIZE AND SUMMARIZE

*"How can a young man keep his way pure? By guarding it according to your word." (Psalm 119:9)*

**We've been studying Colossians 3 for almost four weeks now!** The Holy Spirit has opened God's Word for us as we've slowed down to study it. Now it's time to look back over our notes. What have we learned? What can we do with it all? How will it change our lives? Today let's go back and *summarize* what we've learned.

**Assignment: Read Colossians 3.**

*Start a new page of notes.* Write the numbers 1 through 26 down the left-hand side of the page, leaving a couple lines between each number. These numbers represent each of the twenty-six lessons we have completed (or that some of you are still hoping to complete!).

*Review your notes* from the past month of studying Colossians. Prayerfully think about what you have observed and recorded.

For each lesson, write a *one or two-sentence summary* of what you observed and what God taught you in that lesson. What particular truth stood out to you? What new insights did you gain? (This may take more time than you have in one day. Tomorrow is catch-up day. You'll have more time to finish then, if you need it.)

*Day 27: Organize and Summarize*

When you've finished, *read back through your summary statements*. Do you see any repeated themes or instructions? Can you write *one overall summary statement for the entire chapter*? If you want, write some of these notes in your Bible, so you'll be able to review them when you read Colossians 3 again in the future.

On Day 29, we'll come back to these notes one more time.

*"I will delight in your statutes; I will not forget your word." (Psalm 119:16)*

# DAY 28:
# CATCH UP OR WORD STUDY

**It's catch-up day!** Take some time to finish up a lesson or two, if you've fallen behind. Or finish yesterday's assignment, if it required more time than you had to complete it.

I've sure enjoyed working through this study on Colossians with you. We're almost done with our 30-day study challenge! I hope it's blessed you as much as it has me.

If you *want* an additional assignment, read the entire book of Colossians, marking every reference to "thanks" and its synonyms. We've already done this in Chapter 3 in Lesson 22. Answer these same questions for the rest of the chapter:

- *Why* are we to be thankful?
- *What* are we to be thankful *for*?
- *Who* are we to be thankful *to*?
- *Who* are we to be thankful *with*?
- *Who* are we to be thankful *through*?
- *How* are we to demonstrate and express our thankfulness?
- *How* does thankfulness affect the message of the entire book of Colossians?

# DAY 29:

# CHILDREN

*"All Scripture is breathed out by God and profitable for teaching, for reproof, for correction, and for training in righteousness, that the man of God may be complete, equipped for every good work." (2 Timothy 3:16-17)*

*All* Scripture is profitable for teaching, for reproof, for correction, and for training in righteousness. That means *Colossians 3* is profitable for all those things. My prayer is that our month-long study of this chapter has taught and reproved and corrected and trained us in righteous living.

Look again at those verses from 2 Timothy. Why is God's inspired Word profitable for all these things? So *"that the man of God may be complete, equipped for every good work."* As God teaches us from His Word, He is graciously equipping us for the work He has given us to do.

God has given many of us the good work of raising godly children for His kingdom. Our study in Colossians should better equip us for that work! Let's take a few minutes today to purposefully think about Colossians 3 as it relates to the good work of parenting.

**Assignment: Read Colossians 3 one more time!** Then review your summary notes from Lesson 27. As you read and review, ask yourself these two questions:

1. *What* can I take from this passage that will better equip me to *serve as a godly mother?*

2. What from this passage can I use to *teach, reprove, correct, and train my children?*

Write down at least a half dozen *specific answers* to these questions. Here are some examples:

- As a mother, I should set my mind "on things above" when training my children. Rather than making earthly activities (like sports, good grades, even healthy cooking) a *priority,* my *primary* concern should be to point them to Jesus and train them in godly living.

- I should help "the Word of Christ dwell in [my children] richly with all wisdom" by reading the Bible with them in times of leisure, and when disciplining, and by singing God-centered songs with them throughout the day.

- I should help them understand that when they obey me, they are pleasing *Jesus.*

Pray for *wisdom* as you think about these questions. Pray for *creativity* to teach your children the truths of Scripture in a winsome and effective way. Pray for *discipline and perseverance* to act on these insights, and pray for a *grateful love for Jesus* that will overflow in humble, godly service to your family.

*"Whatever you do, work heartily, as for the Lord and not for men, knowing that from the Lord you will receive the inheritance as your reward.* **You are serving the Lord Christ.***" (Colossians 3:23-24)*

# DAY 30:

# DOING

Our last day! God teaches us as we dig into His Word. How do we keep from *forgetting* what He's taught us? How do we actively put into *practice* all that we've learned?

Here are some ideas!

- **Share what you've learned with someone else.** Share some new insights with a friend, tell your husband what you learned in the study, or show a friend or one of your children how to use these methods of study.

- Take the methods you've learned and **continue to use them to study another passage.** Use the instructions on page 80-82 to give you some ideas as you finish studying Colossians or start studying another Bible passage. Look for patterns and repeated words and mark what you believe will help you grow to better understand the passage.

- **Write goals.** Be specific. What *actions* will you take as a result of what you have learned? In what ways will you *think* differently? Pick just one or two goals, so you won't be overwhelmed. You can always come back, review the lesson, and write some new goals when you've reached your first ones.

- **Be accountable.** *Share your goals* with someone else. Ask her to hold you accountable. If you're committing to daily Bible study, email her when you've finished your study each day.

- **Reread the chapter at least once a week.** Or download it onto your iPhone or MP3 player and listen to it each week.

- **Memorize the entire chapter.** (It's not as hard as it sounds, especially if you've been reading it all month. I have managed to memorize the whole chapter, and I'll bet my brain is a lot older and more worn out than most of yours!) I used *Memorize His Word* to help me learn it. Now I would use the ScriptureTyper app on my phone, but there are many ways to help yourself accomplish such a goal. Go back and check out Day 20's lesson for a few ideas to help you memorize. Look online for more.

- **Read *Jesus + Nothing = Everything,*** by Tullian Tchividjian. This book was sitting on my shelf, waiting for me to read it, for several months. My daughter, Susannah, finally decided to read it, and we found out its message is based on the book of *Colossians!* It looks like it would make a great follow-up for our Colossians study!

- **Listen to Pastor Tchividjian's sermon series on Colossians** at http://www.crpc.org/resources/sermons/series/colossians. Bethany, another of our daughters, tracked this one down, and she says the sermons are amazing! I've downloaded them to listen to in the car. They can also be watched or listened to on your computer.

- Ask for a **wide margin Bible** or **Inductive Study Bible** for your birthday or Christmas or just because! (See Appendix A for ideas.)

# Appendix A:
# Materials for Your Study

- **Colored pencils**

  You can mark in your Bible with just a couple pens of different colors if you mark in a variety of ways (single and double underline, box, circle, dotted line, initials, etc.). But if you can afford it, it's nice to use an assortment of colored pencils and fine-point colored pens.

  Prismacolor soft core (Premier) colored pencils are an excellent choice. These soft lead pencils mark thin Bible pages easily without marring them, and the colors are rich and vibrant. They're a bit expensive, but you don't need a big set (twelve is plenty), and they're well worth the cost.

  Be sure you don't buy Prismacolor *Verithin* pencils. They are hard lead, which will not work well. They and other cheaper colored pencils are hard to see, and their harder leads damage the fragile paper in most Bibles.

  Here's another idea for keeping your children busy and happy while you study. Put your box of pencils (or another set) out where the kids can reach them, set out a couple inexpensive, but good quality Dover coloring books, and share your pencils while you study. Or get brave and let the kids draw some simple illustrations in your Bible along with you!

- **Black and colored pens**

  Use a fine or micro-point pen for writing words and drawing little pictures. My favorite is a Uniball Micro Point roller ball pen. The ink does occasionally show through the page a bit. If that bothers you, keep experimenting until you find a pen you like. Ballpoint pens don't show through as much, but I like the darker, sharp lines of the roller ball pen.

- **Bible**

  Ideally, it's nice to use a Bible with wide margins that allow room for writing lists and other observations. If you don't have room in your Bible, or if you just can't bring yourself to mark up your Bible, print out the passage you want to study. Double-space the text and leave lots of room on the page for notes. Put it in a notebook and mark away! I personally think it's really nice to have a Bible with all my own personal markings and drawings in it — kind of like my own "illuminated" Bible. I have printed out portions to mark, but they are not nearly as easy to pull out and review as the ones in my Bible.

  The Bible I have used for years is the *International Inductive Study Bible.* It was published by Harvest House in 1993. The translation is the New American Standard Bible. (This Bible is also going to be available as the *New Inductive Study Bible* in August 2013 in the ESV!)

  My old edition has nice big margins for notes, and nice big print, which leaves more space for marking the text. The big print was also nice when my little guys were looking over my shoulder and wanted to read what I was reading. Newer hardback and leather-bound editions of this Bible are also available. They are smaller (the 1993 edition is a big 7-1/2" x 9-1/2" x 2") and costs less than the 1993 edition, but it does have smaller margins and smaller type.

  Each book in this inductive study Bible is preceded by some historical background and suggestions for ways to approach the text – key words to watch for, things to think about, themes to observe, charts to organize your observations. The notes are designed to help you study the Bible for yourself. This is the Bible that really got me excited about studying the Bible!

  Some other wide-margin options are:

  - *The New International Study Bible* (English Standard Version available August 2013)

- *The ESV Single Column Legacy Bible* has nice wide margins.

- *The ESV Single Column Journaling Bible,* includes lines for notes in the outside margins. (Be sure to download a preview of the interior!)

- *The Notetaker's Bible* is available in KJV.

- *The Wide Margin Loose Leaf Reference Bible* is bound in a 3-ring binder, available in KJV, ESV, NASB, and NIV.

- **Paper**

  This doesn't need to be anything fancy, unless you want it to be. A few sheets of notebook paper or a small notepad will be sufficient.

- **A place to store your materials**

  This might be a desk, or perhaps you will prefer a basket or other portable receptacle.

# APPENDIX B:
# IDEAS FOR MARKING IN YOUR BIBLE

I would like to explain some of the markings I use, with the hope that you might find this helpful in your own Bible study. Don't try to duplicate these markings. You may find some that are useful to you. Use them; but make up a system that works for you and that you will remember.

If you're the type of person who will feel compelled to try to use these exact same markings, you should just skim this portion of the book, and move on! You'll get frustrated trying to remember my system and miss out on a lot of what God wants to say to you as you study.

My own system is actually pretty flexible. I have some specific colors I tend to associate with certain ideas (and I will explain some of those below), but some markings change, depending on what passage I'm studying. Sometimes a particular passage will have a repeated word or idea, and I just start circling it in a consistent way that will draw my attention to it. My goal is simply to aid my own study.

Anyone trying to translate my markings as a consistent system or "language" would be frustrated. If you looked at several different sections in my Bible, you would see that markings are not always consistent. This is partly due to the fact that my markings span a period of over twenty years. Sometimes I just forget how I marked a word in one passage, and mark it differently in another.

Differences also occur because one passage may have particular words repeated over and over, but they are not words that I consistently mark throughout my Bible. I might use a purple pen to mark the word "faith" in Hebrews 11 and then use the same marking in a different passage for a different word. I do have some words that I consistently mark in the same way, but the rest of the time I just do whatever I think will work for me as I'm reading.

Here's a sampling of the main markings I use, but remember – these are just ideas. The most effective system for you is the one you design. Borrow ideas you like; adapt or reject the rest. Your system will grow as you continue to study.

I try to use markings that I can associate with things, to help me remember. As I assign a particular marking to a word, I write it on a 3x5 card (or any handy scrap of paper) to keep in my Bible.

- I mark references to **God** with a yellow pencil. In my drawings, I use a yellow triangle to represent God. I also color any other images representing God yellow. For example, if I'm illustrating a verse that mentions God drawing me "out of many waters," I draw a hand lifting a little stick person out of the water, and I color the hand yellow. Then I know when I look at the drawing that it is illustrating God saving me. I remember to use yellow to represent God because yellow reminds me of His glory.

- I mark references to **Jesus** with yellow and then add an upright red cross over the word.

- A slanting red cross marks words related to the **cross, salvation,** and **deliverance.**

- I underline **actions**:
  - God's actions (or what the writer is asking God to do) with blue – what He has done, what He is doing, what He will do.
  - The writer's actions with green
  - The reader/listener's actions (or commands given to him) with red.
  - When doing this I use a wiggly line for past actions, a solid line for present actions, and a dotted line for future actions.

- References to **righteous, upright, blameless,** etc., get marked with green. (I chose green for righteousness because it makes me think of the righteous man who is like a tree planted by the water in Psalm 1.)

- References to the **wicked** are marked with a black W.

- **Sin** and its synonyms are underlined with a wiggly black line.

- References to **world, earth**, and **creation** get marked with a solid blue circle. (I associate that with the photos of our blue earth in space.)

- The word **king** and other references to royalty get marked with an orange crown. (The orange makes me think of gold.)

- **Parts of the body** are usually illustrated with simple line drawings (i.e., hand, arm, foot).

- I draw a red "J" over the words **judge, judgment, just**, and **justice**, along with their synonyms.

- **Love, lovingkindness**, and other references related to love are marked with a red heart.

- I circle in black the words **all** and **every**. This often proves to be a useful word to pay attention to as I read.

- I circle words like **for** and **because** with a black pen and fill the circle in with a red pencil. These words link the thoughts that come before them with the thoughts that follow them. They point us to reasons. Marking the words helps me pay attention and make those connections, and filling the circle in with red helps the marking stand out on the page so I can easily pinpoint the reasons that are given in the passage.

- **Therefore** gets underlined with a wiggly line with an arrow on the right hand end, pointing to what follows.

- I circle with a red pen the word **but** and synonyms, such as however.

- I draw two slanted lines with a brown pen through the word **like** and **as** to draw my attention to comparisons, such as we see in Psalm 37:6, *"He will bring forth your righteousness as the light, and your justice as the noonday."*

- I draw a red box around verses that I particularly want to draw attention to or remember.

- A red question mark in the margin draws my attention to any **questions** asked in the text.

- A blue box marks **promises**.

- I number **lists** within a passage, such as the list of what we are to put off in Colossians 3. Then I usually write the entire list in the margin.

- I draw pictures where I think it will help me remember the concept better. When I'm inspired or just wanting to pray about what I've read, I color the pictures. This is certainly not necessary; I just like doing it and it gives me time to think about what I'm ilustrating.

In some places, like the Psalms, I mark a lot. In others, like Old Testament narratives, I mark words less, but make more notes in the margins about chronology and truths that are displayed in the stories. Sometimes I just mark all the verbs in a passage to see patterns, or all the commands.

How will you mark words and phrases in your Bible (or printed-out text, if you prefer to not mark in your actual Bible)?

The best marking system is going to be the one you custom-design. You need:

- A plan that you can remember

- Colors and pictures that you can associate with particular words and ideas.

What will help you think harder about what you are reading? What marks or pictures will help, rather than distract, you as you read? You can come up with your own marking system as you read. Keep a 3x5 card in your Bible and note your symbols and marking methods as you read.

# APPENDIX C:

# How to Make Time When You Have Small Children

Getting up just a little earlier in the morning is one way to make time for Bible reading and study. However, for mothers who are caring for tiny ones during the night, an early rising may not be practical. If you're a mother with several little children, you may have trouble coming up with enough energy to get up any earlier than they already do, and it may be challenging finding even five minutes of time to concentrate in a day.

Keep a log of your time use for two or three days. Try to record every activity. Don't leave out the little bits of time that might get spent on non-essentials or Facebook or puttering. When you are done, look carefully at how you use your time. Are there moments you can redeem somehow? Can you come up with just five minutes – maybe one minute at a time throughout the day? Ask your husband or a trusted friend to look over your time log, too. They may have some suggestions.

Then let's think creatively about how you can spend time in the Word during the day or even in the middle of the night!

- Can you establish a quiet hour during the day when everyone is either napping or sitting quietly on their beds with books or quiet toys? Use at least part of this time to read and pray.

- Keep your Bible at your nursing station and read while you feed Baby during the night.

- Post verses on cards throughout the house. Meditate on them while you cook, while you load the washer, or while you fix your hair. Assign an older child the task of copying verses onto cards for you, and change the verses regularly.

- Place small Bibles in strategic places throughout the house – the bathroom, near the toddler's potty chair, in your purse, in the car. Take advantage of the brief opportunities that present themselves. If you have children with you, read aloud to them and involve them in what you are learning.

- Purchase an audio version of the Bible on CD, or download one onto a smartphone or MP3 player. Play it while you exercise, while you groom yourself in the morning, while you and the children work on quiet projects in the dining room or family room.

- Read a short passage aloud with your children at lunch time or before naps.

- Ask your husband if he would be willing to care for the children in order to give you at least a few minutes alone each day. Or perhaps he or a friend or family member could give you at least a couple hours for quiet study at a coffee shop each week.

- Ask your husband to read to you while you get ready in the morning or while you cook. You'll get the added benefit of time together and conversations about what you've read.

- Play worship music and Psalms set to music during the day.

- Sing the Psalms as you work and care for your children. Teach them to your children and have them join in with you!

# APPENDIX D:

# HOW TO STUDY ON YOUR OWN

You can take the basic approach of this study on Colossians 3 and apply it to other passages on your own. Here are the basic steps:

We can summarize what we have been doing in this book with three words:

1. Observe
2. Interpret
3. Apply

These are the basic steps in the inductive study method. Inductive reasoning collects information and draws conclusions from what has been observed. In a similar way, inductive Bible study makes careful observations and then draws conclusions about the meaning of a passage based on those observations (with the revealing help of the Holy Spirit and the aid of commentaries and other resources).

First, **we observe**. We find out what the passage says. We do this by investigating, much like a detective would. We ask questions and look for answers. We carefully observe, mark, and record what we find.

We ask the traditional questions of a news reporter in order to learn all we can from the text. Who? What? Where? When? Why?

We look for:

- Repeated words
- Questions in the text
- Reasons given (words like "because" and "for")
- Lists within the text
- Contrasts ("but", "rather", etc.)
- Comparisons ("like", "as")
- Conclusions ("therefore", "so", "thus", etc.)
- Conditional statements ("If...then")

As we observe the text, underlining, circling, and marking the words in unique ways helps us see patterns and themes.

Next, after observing what a passage says, **we find out what it means**.

- We look at the passage and its meaning within its context. What book of the Bible is this passage in? What is the purpose of that book? We are careful to not take a passage out of context in order to make it say what we want it to say.

- We interpret the passage's meaning in light of the rest of Scripture. What does the rest of the Bible have to say about the subject in this passage or the conclusion I am coming to? (Looking at commentaries as described below may help you with this step.)

- We think about the literary form of the passage. Is it historical, poetic, or prophetic? Is it a letter written to a group of believers? This will affect how we interpret the passage. (Again, see instructions related to commentaries below, if you need help.)

- We prayerfully review and organize our observations to help us understand what the passage means.

- We look to the teaching of others. Before I draw my final conclusions, I also refer to at least one reliable, doctrinally sound commentary. I do this *after* I have completed most of my own observations and summary, because part of the beauty of inductive study is that the reader is interacting directly with the text, not with what someone else has said about it.

  However, I am a sinful being who can be easily blinded to my own sin. I am also part of the body of Christ, the Church. My knowledge is limited. My heart is deceitful. The teaching and commentary of other mature believers can help me better understand a passage's real meaning and its relevance to my life. Reading a short commentary on the passage after our observations will help steer us from faulty conclusions or misinterpretations.

Last, **we apply what we've learned**. This is the whole point of our study. We don't just study to know more. We study so we can obey.

We can ask ourselves questions like:

- What can I learn from this passage?

- How does this passage apply to my life?

- How does this passage apply to my present circumstances?

- What is God calling me to do with what I have learned?

I find it useful at this point in my study to write down *specific actions* I am going to take or *specific changes* I am seeking to make, with the Holy Spirit's help, as a result of studying the passage.

For more information on the inductive study method as outlined by Precept Ministries International, go to:

http://precept.org/about_inductive_bible_study.

For more *Busy Mamas Bible Studies,* be sure to join me at the *Doorposts of Your House* blog (www.doorposts.com/blog). I occasionally host a month-long study, with one five-minute assignment delivered to you each day. The studies also include a Facebook group where you can interact with other ladies who are all studying the same passage along with you.